FOLK BALLADS
for Young Actors

John Jacob Niles

Helen Louise Smith

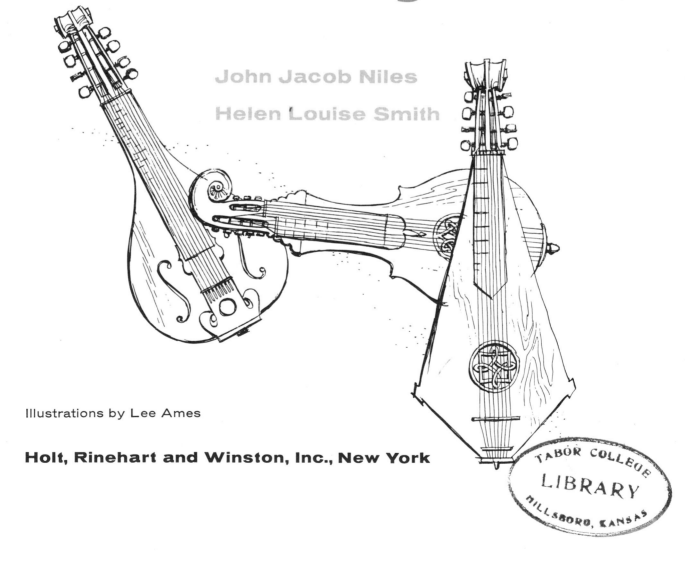

Illustrations by Lee Ames

Holt, Rinehart and Winston, Inc., New York

Acknowledgements

We wish to express our appreciation to the following authors and publishers for permission to use copyrighted material:

Doubleday & Company, Inc. for "Mice" by Rose Fyleman, from FIFTY-ONE NEW NURSERY RHYMES by Rose Fyleman. Copyright 1932 by Doubleday & Company, Inc. Reprinted by permission of the publishers and of The Society of Authors as the Literary Representative of the Estate of the late Miss Rose Fyleman. "The Spring" by Rose Fyleman, from THE FAIRY GREEN by Rose Fyleman. Copyright 1923 by George H. Doran Company. Reprinted by permission of Doubleday & Company, Inc. and of The Society of Authors as the Literary Representative of the Estate of the late Miss Rose Fyleman.

E. P. Dutton & Co., Inc. for "Grandfather Frog" by Louise Seaman Bechtel, "The House of the Mouse" by Lucy Sprague Mitchell, and "Jump or Jiggle" by Evelyn Beyer, from ANOTHER HERE AND NOW STORY BOOK by Lucy Sprague Mitchell. Copyright 1937 by E. P. Dutton & Co., Inc. Reprinted by permission of the publishers.

Lothrop, Lee & Shepard Co., Inc. for "Wild Beasts" by Evaleen Stein, from CHILD SONGS OF CHEER by Evaleen Stein, and used by permission of Lothrop, Lee & Shepard Co., Inc.

G. Schirmer, Inc. for permission to use the four ballads in this book.

Library of Congress Catalog Card Number 62-12308
16079-0112

Printed in the United States of America

8-28-64

Table of Contents

Authors' Foreword

Folk Ballads for Young Actors is designed to provide materials and suggestions for experiences in creative dramatics. The ballads in this collection have been sung to many young audiences, but they have never before been published in a form so immediately useful to teachers and parents. The stories for introducing the songs are original and appear only in this publication.

The plan of presentation for each folk ballad includes a story for the teacher to tell, preferably in her own words, as a means of building interest, stirring imagery, and stimulating a response to the song itself. The stories have been written simply but vividly, and the teacher's own expressive voice and face will capture the children's attention.

Teaching suggestions are provided in each unit for the teacher who is inexperienced in the leadership of creative dramatics. Certain techniques are necessary to lead the children into creative dramatic experiences. Creative dramatics may be approached through different media: storytelling, music and rhythmic movement, poetry and choral reading, pantomime and characterization with or without dialogue, or through experiences in art with simple finger painting or free crayon work. In using any of these approaches the teacher should constantly strive for individual responses. As the children respond and exchange thoughts and feelings they become alive with a kind of free-flowing energy. Their bodies express the rhythms of nature or the typical movements and postures of animals.

The teacher is part of every situation in creative dramatics. She is not a "director" — she is a guide, moving in to offer encouraging words when the momentum lags and withdrawing when the children "take hold." The teacher is a leader who is able to keep the atmosphere open and fluid, drawing forth a spontaneous response from the children's own thinking.

The folk ballad as a source of pure imagery is almost inexhaustible. Singing and rhyming words can play an important role in the total language program for young children, giving an opportunity for the correct and distinct pronunciation of words, the stress on vowel sounds, and the rhythmic flow of syllables and words. Humorous folk songs in particular, with their nonsense syllables sung repetitiously, provide a group activity in which every child uses his voice freely as he rolls the sounds over his tongue. The child with speech difficulty loses his inhibitions in the group response. Here is another means of oral language development.

In some cases, the creative dramatics experience may provide therapy for a child with articulatory disorders. Simply to make speech enjoyable through games and techniques at the child's level is recommended by speech therapists.

Either during the same period in which the story is told, or perhaps more successfully after a short lapse or even a day, the recording of the ballad could be played to give the group a chance to recognize the story in a new guise. Upon hearing the recording, the children will probably want to learn the words and the tune immediately. Since the folk singer requires freedom of interpretation, and since this freedom (rubato) adds to the child's enjoyment of the song, it is suggested that the recording be played several times before the children attempt to sing with it.

The recording found in this book is to be used for helping the pupils interpret the ballads. The songs on the recording should be used one at a time. The primary purpose of the recording is to motivate the children to work out the details of the drama they create. If the teacher prefers to provide the kind of direct teaching which a recording cannot do, she may play the piano accompaniments and sing the ballads herself. Chord letters are indicated for chording instruments such as the guitar. The autoharp may be played with songs in certain keys.

The stories, songs, and suggestions in this book contain no magic. The test is in the using of them to stimulate the creative power within the group. The teacher provides the spark by asking questions and using words that "free" the emotional and intellectual resources of the children. Discussion between the teacher and the group is the secret to the development of creative dramatics. The children's natural bent toward make-believe and drama in everyday life is easily led by a line of questioning that is nondirective.

The techniques suggested in this book are intended primarily for *informal drama.* The children provide the action and dialogue spontaneously, preferably without attempting to copy or structure a performance. The object is not to perfect a drama, but to encourage individual and group participation. Suggestions are "tried out" through bodily movement and vocal expression in speech and song. Thoughts and feelings motivate from *within,* in the attempt for a mental and physical identification with the figures in the story or song. The teacher urges and guides from *without,* with words and questions that pull from the young actors their own deeper responses.

After children have been drawn into the creative dramatic experiences that are suggested in this book, it might be rewarding and appropriate to extend those experiences into a play for presentation. These plays would be ideal to present before school assemblies, parent groups, and other classes.

There is a place for singing in the reading program of the elementary school. Singing increases the child's auditory memory span, builds his vocabulary, and gives deeper intellectual and emotional concepts to word meanings. For children who are slow to read, there is a kinesthetic and emotional help from rote songs with strong rhythmic impulses. The sound in this case precedes the sight. There are many ways by which music may aid the developmental reading program at any grade level.

Thus, folk ballads, when carried one step further and used as creative dramatics, become a valuable help to the truly creative teacher. In folk ballads there is a challenge of myriad changes of emphasis and inflection. In much the same way, there is a challenge for parents and teachers to observe the variety of ideas and interpretations which come from children who participate in creative dramatics.

The Frog in the Spring

Once upon a time, a big green frog lived in a spring beside a big white house. Since he could live in or out of water, he loved to hop up to the house and watch the children play. Sometimes, when they heard him sing, they would try to find and catch Mr. Frog, but he was too sly for them. He would hide in the bottom of an old green well behind the house. Since Mr. Frog did not have much to do, he spent most of his time singing and catching insects. When he sang, it sounded like this, "Twiddle, widdle, widdle, widdle, widdle, widdle, widdle, wing."

One day Mr. Frog bounced up the hill to watch the children play. When he started to sing, he discovered that he was too hoarse to make a sound. He tried and tried, but he had sung so much that he could not croak above a whisper. He jumped into the old well and got a drink of cool water, thinking this might clear his throat. When he came out he tried to sing again, but he was still hoarse. This made him very unhappy. He could not play hide and seek with the children unless he could sing, "Twiddle, widdle, widdle, widdle, widdle, widdle, widdle, wing."

As he sat beside the well looking very sad, a little girl-mouse came tripping across the grass. The mouse was carrying a bucket, so Mr. Frog thought that she must be coming to fetch some water from the well.

"Hello," she said shyly. "Why do you look so sad, Mr. Frog?"

Mr. Frog croaked in a whisper, "I am sad because I am too hoarse to sing. I usually sing all day long, but today I am too hoarse to sing a note."

"Oh Mr. Frog," she replied cheerfully, "I have just been to the sassafras bush. Let me make you a cup of sassafras tea."

After Mr. Frog drank his cup of tea, he tried to sing again. To his delight he could sing, "Twiddle, widdle, widdle, widdle, widdle, widdle, widdle, wee." He hopped and hopped and sang and sang. This made him happy again. "Oh Miss Mouse, thank you so much. I can never repay you for that delicious cup of sassafras tea!"

Miss Mouse nodded and quietly started on her way. Suddenly Mr. Frog realized what a pretty little mouse she was. He ran after her and said, "Please don't go. Stay and talk with me awhile. What is your name?"

"My name is Bess," she sighed. She thought he was wonderful because he had such a good voice.

"Twiddle, widdle, widdle, widdle, widdle, widdle, widdle, wess," sang Mr. Frog, "it is nice to have you here with me, Bess. I have been lonely here all by myself, with only the children at the big house to keep me company. Will you please marry me and stay forever? We can live here in the old green well."

Bess liked his singing, his pretty green coat, and his great big eyes. Finally, she decided that Mr. Frog would make a good husband. "Yes, I'll marry you," she said, "but first you will have to ask my mother and father."

Mr. Frog and Bess started across the field to see her parents. As Mr. Frog hopped along, the grass tickled his stomach. He wondered why anybody would live in a dry field of stubble and briars. Mr. Frog was in a hurry to get out of that field, but Bess thought that he was eager to see her parents, so she ran along without complaining. Finally, Mr. Frog and Bess came to her home in the field. Her mother and father were polite but not really friendly to Mr. Frog. Mr. and Mrs. Mouse were not at all pleased with the idea of Bess marrying a frog. They simply told Bess that frogs were not nice. Bess was very hurt. She replied that frogs were just as nice as mice. Then Mr. Frog nodded his head way down in his thick green neck and said, "Twiddle, widdle, widdle, widdle, widdle, widdle, widdle, wice!" When Mr. and Mrs. Mouse heard that wonderful bass voice, they agreed to let their daughter marry Mr. Frog. In fact, they were delighted to hear that Mr. Frog was being considered for a leading role in the Briarfield Opera Company.

Mr. Frog and Bess were married, and off they went to live at the bottom of the old green well. Bess was very happy at first. Before long, however, she began to be sad. It was very damp and dreary in the bottom of the well, and she often had to wade in water up to her chin. She began to think about her nice dry, grassy home in the woods. Sometimes she even wished she could be a maid again! But when Mr. Frog sang, "Twiddle, widdle, widdle, widdle, widdle, widdle, win," she knew she loved him and would never wish to be single again.

Teaching Suggestions for "The Frog in the Spring"

This ballad probably grew out of the story about a beautiful queen who wanted to marry a man from another country. The queen's subjects did not like the idea. They could not speak out against the queen's wishes, but they were irritated and grumbled among themselves. They decided to write a song about a wedding between a frog and a mouse. The song pointed out some of the problems that would come out of this strange wedding. The people hoped that their queen would hear the song and understand the implications.

The men who write history are not clear about it, but it is believed that the queen did not marry the man from the foreign country. In fact, she never married at all. It is interesting to wonder if the ballad caused the queen to call off the marriage. Perhaps she never intended to marry, but the story made an interesting song that has several variants.

How to Dramatize

First efforts at creative dramatics may seem crude and undisciplined, but the suggestions given by the authors of *Folk Ballads for Young Actors* follow a teaching plan of step-by-step motivation.

Through the storytelling period, the teacher will be building interest. The children will enjoy discussing the words that may be new to them, such as "spring," "well," and "sassafras." City children love the word "sassafras," although they may never completely appreciate its meaning until they smell the aroma of the sassafras root boiling on the stove. Creative dramatics will bring them close to ways of living that may be remote and very different from their own lives.

Having heard the recording of the song, it should take little more than the question, "Would you boys and girls like to act out the story of this song?" to get a very positive response. Once the children are in a circle for a discussion period, the teacher or parent will get eager responses to a few selected questions:

Who are the characters in this story?
What does a frog look like?
What sounds does a frog make?
How does a mouse move?
Do mice and frogs eat different kinds of food?
Did you ever drink water out of a spring? or a well?
Why did the frog drink the tea made of sassafras?

No doubt, at this point a few children will have demonstrated how a frog leaps and how a mouse moves along the ground!

After the children have heard the song on the recording, having listened several times *without singing,* they may speak the words as choral speech, just to make sure that everyone knows them. Children will enjoy the tongue-twister, "Twiddle, widdle, widdle, widdle, widdle, widdle, widdle, wing." They will enjoy finding the rhyming words, too, such as spring-wing, free-wee, Bess-wess, nice-wice, tell-well, and chin-win. The words of this song will give children an opportunity to master the sounds of the t's, d's, and w's. Teachers may find this song very effective in working with pupils who have speech difficulties.

Once this much has been accomplished as background, a few of the children, or maybe the entire group, will be ready to sing freely and interpretively when the record is played. The teacher may have played the song on the piano, using the simplified accompaniment in this book.

The children may then begin to offer suggestions for the setting and properties. Here again, the teacher should be guided by simplicity and the child's imagination. The spring may be a circle outlined on the floor with string or rope. The home of the mouse could be an old orange crate, or just the corner of the room. The green well might be a ring of small chairs, with their backs turned inward — or even the children themselves may form a circle to "house" the frog and his bride!

The children are thinking, improvising, originating; therefore, it may be necessary to play the story many times. Everyone will want a chance to be the leading characters. Those not taking a part can be the chorus or the audience. For example, the chorus could join in together to sing the words, "Twiddle, widdle, widdle, widdle, widdle,

widdle, widdle, wing." There are various ways to coordinate the music and action in these ballads.

In some instances it might be best to play the record or have a chorus sing the entire song before the action begins. Or, the ballad may be sung verse by verse as the plot is developed.

Costuming is not always necessary in creative dramatics. Body movements will express the characters sufficiently. However, if costuming is desired, there are many ways to "dress up" as the characters. The child playing the frog could wear a green coat, or simply have a piece of green cloth thrown over his shoulders. For the wedding, Miss Mouse could carry a bunch of imitation flowers and wear something resembling a veil. The important factor is that every child discover the fun of being an "animal character."

Each of the ballads in this book offers an opportunity for the teacher to correlate creative dramatics with other subjects in the curriculum. It would be simple to develop a unit of study using any one of these ballads as the core.

In this particular ballad, discussion and study of the habits of frogs and mice would make an interesting science lesson. In the intermediate grades, this ballad may even lead to a study of various sources of water, such as springs and wells. In the field of social studies, it would provide an excellent springboard for discussion of environments and how people with different backgrounds have different ways of living and social customs. It has already been suggested that the children will enjoy finding the rhyming words. This may lead to choral readings or the writing of simple rhymes and verses in connection with the language arts program. The ballad also gives children opportunities for creative and artistic expression through the making of simple costumes for frogs and mice. Color crayons and finger paints may also be used in graphic representations of the animals in this story.

Related Material

The Spring

A little mountain spring I found
That fell into a pool;
I made my hands into a cup
And caught the sparkling water up —
It tasted fresh and cool.

A solemn little frog I spied
Upon the rocky brim;
He looked so boldly in my face,
I'm certain that he thought the place
Belonged by rights to him.

Rose Fyleman

Mice

I think mice
Are rather nice.

Their tails are long,
Their faces small,
They haven't any
Chins at all.
Their ears are pink,
Their teeth are white,
They run about
The house at night.
They nibble things
They shouldn't touch
And no one seems
To like them much.

But I think mice
Are nice.

Rose Fyleman

Grandfather Frog

Fat green frog sits by the pond,
Big frog, bull frog, grandfather frog.
Croak-croak-croak.
Shuts his eye, opens his eye,
Rolls his eye, winks his eye,
Waiting for
A little fat fly.
Croak, croak.
I go walking down by the pond,
I want to see the big green frog.
I want to stare right into his eye,
Rolling, winking, funny old eye.
But oh! he hears me coming by.
Croak-croak —
SPLASH!!

Louise Seaman Bechtel

The House of the Mouse

The house of the mouse
is a wee little house,
a green little house in the grass,
which big clumsy folk
may hunt and may poke
and still never see as they pass
this sweet little, neat little,
wee little, green little,
cuddle-down hide-away
house in the grass.

Lucy Sprague Mitchell

The Frog in the Spring

1. There was a frog lived in a spring, Twid - dle, wid - dle, wid - dle wid - dle wid - dle, wid - dle, wid - dle, wing. He was so hoarse he could not sing, Twid - dle, wid - dle, wid - dle, wid - dle, wid - dle, wid - dle, wid - dle, wing.

10

2. He took a swig of sassy-fras tea,
   Twiddle, widdle, widdle, widdle, widdle,
   Widdle, widdle, wee.
   And then his singing was fine and free,
   Twiddle, widdle, widdle, widdle, widdle,
   Widdle, widdle, wee.

3. He courted a mouse and her name was Bess,
   Twiddle, widdle, widdle, widdle, widdle,
   Widdle, widdle, wess.
   And he courted and he courted till she said, "Yes,"
   Twiddle, widdle, widdle, widdle, widdle,
   Widdle, widdle, wess.

4. Her Maw and Paw says, "Frogs ain't nice,"
   Twiddle, widdle, widdle, widdle, widdle,
   Widdle, widdle, wice.
   She said, "They're quite as nice as mice,"
   Twiddle, widdle, widdle, widdle, widdle,
   Widdle, widdle, wicc.

5. So they were married, folks do tell,
   Twiddle, widdle, widdle, widdle, widdle,
   Widdle, widdle, well.
   And they lived at the bottom of the old green well,
   Twiddle, widdle, widdle, widdle, widdle,
   Widdle, widdle, well.

6. Then Mousie waded in water to her chin,
   Twiddle, widdle, widdle, widdle, widdle,
   Widdle, widdle, win.
   And she often wished she was a maid again,
   Singing twiddle, widdle, widdle, widdle,
   Widdle, widdle, win.

The Story of Noah

Many years ago, a man by the name of Noah decided to build a ship. It was to be a very big ship, made like a long, wide house, three stories high. In those days a ship of this kind was known as an ark. Noah knew that it was going to rain for forty days and forty nights, so he and his sons started to work on the ark. Noah decided to build the ark on the top of a high mountain. He and his sons cut the tallest trees from the forest and hauled them up the mountain. All the neighbors thought Noah was crazy to build such a big ark on top of a mountain so very far from any water. Noah did not seem to mind. He just kept on working.

Noah worked on the ark for many years. Just as he finished it, the skies grew dark with black clouds. Suddenly, there was a flash of lightning and a crack of thunder. Then a heavy rain began to pour from the skies. Within a few days the rivers and lakes were overflowing. As the rains filled the fields and valleys with water, many of the animals left in search of higher ground. The water began creeping up the hills, and all the animals grew frightened. Those that could climb or fly were already gathering in the tallest trees.

"I'm so glad I built my house in this tall tree," said the squirrel to the birds. "I have food stored away, so I'll be safe during the flood."

"I really feel sorry for all those animals who cannot fly," said the hawk. "If the water covers the trees, I'll fly through the air and be safe."

A big bear who was clinging to a tree trunk said to the hawk, "You won't be safe either. You will have to rest sometime — and where would you land?"

"I never thought of that," said the hawk, as he drooped his head. "Not even birds will be safe."

A monkey jumped from tree to tree as the water got higher. He was chattering to himself as he landed in a tall tree with all the birds. "Move over," he said, "this flood is getting serious. I just saw the giraffe wading out of the forest. The water was all the way up to his chin, and that is really deep!"

The wise old owl was excited too. He opened his big eyes and said, "I have a strange feeling that this flood will soon cover all the land and even the trees." He remembered that the eagle had a perch on a very high mountain. "I'll go to the eagle," said the owl. "There may be a good dry place for all of us on that high mountain where the eagle lives."

The owl found the eagle on the mountain top and told him that all the animals were worried about the flood.

"Yes, they should be worried," said the eagle. "I can see water for miles and miles from this mountain top. There is not much land left."

The eagle took the owl by the wing and said, "Let's go see Noah. I've been watching him build a big ark right here on the mountain top. I heard him say that he wanted the ark to be big enough to take care of all the animals and birds when the flood came."

When the owl and the eagle reached the ark, Noah put down his hammer and said, "Go tell all the animals and birds to come here as fast as they can. I have enough food for all of them to live here on the ark until the flood is over."

The owl and the eagle went back and told all their friends to head for the ark. When Noah saw all the animals coming up the mountain, he wondered if he had made the ark big enough. He decided to count the animals two by two as they entered the ark. But the water was rising fast, and the animals became more and more nervous. Noah let the animals come in three by three, then four by four. He decided to let some of them in the window as well as the door. As the animals crowded into the ark, Noah had to smile when he saw a bumblebee coming in with a big bear. The animals were coming in so fast that Noah thought it might be wise to let them in five by five, then six by six, then seven by seven. He had to stop counting and settle a little scuffle when the elephant began to shove the ant. When the animals began to come in eight by eight, Noah yelled, "Shut that gate!" Finally, the last animals came in nine by nine and Noah shouted, "Boys, cut the line!" Soon the water reached the top of the mountain, and the ark floated away.

With all safely aboard, Noah sat down to rest. When he opened his eyes, he found all the animals standing in a circle around him. They were all so glad to be safe that they began to sing, "Who built the ark? Noah built it, Noah built it!" And Noah, his family, and all the animals were happy indeed.

Teaching Suggestions for "The Story of Noah"

This song is a humorous musical setting of the biblical story about Noah and the ark. It probably originated in much the same way as other spirituals that deal with biblical heroes such as Joshua, Elijah, and David.

In the days when showboats plied the Ohio and Mississippi rivers, *The Story of Noah* was a great favorite with minstrel groups. At one time there were as many as fifty verses, involving all kinds of animals, birds, and insects.

How to Dramatize

This ballad will fit in very well and add a new dimension to study units or projects involving animals. The teacher may wish to carry out all of the usual correlations with arts and crafts — the making of papier-mâché animals, or animals modeled with clay or plastic. Some children may want to make puppets using original conceptions of the animals. The ballad should also provide correlations with poetry and prose (the A. A. Milne stories, or poems by Emily Dickinson, or poems by William Jay Smith in his collections entitled *Boy Blue's Book of Beasts* and *Laughing Time*).

The humor of the word pictures in the song *The Story of Noah* can be caught quickly from the first listening to the record. The teacher and the children may want to discuss word pictures that are funny: the cow chewing on a caraway bun, the bear hugging the bumblebee, the elephant shoving the ant. As the recording is played a second and third time, the children will begin to see other pictures. (The teacher may want to take quick notes on the ideas that the children express. Some of the ideas may be used later as a musical play is created.)

The children will not keep silent very long on this ballad, so they should be allowed to sing along as best they can with the tricky rhythm and tongue-curling words. Do not be surprised if certain words, in the fast moving tune, come out as *Norah* for Noah, and *rhinosaurous* for rhinoceros. We are not concerned here with teaching children to spell or pronounce each word precisely. We are concerned, however, with the humor of word sounds as they sharpen imagery through the interaction of sound (tune and musical patterns) and kinesthetics (action in rhythms and reaction based on thoughtful characterizations). Allow the children to demonstrate individually and collectively how they "see" all of the animals going into the ark. At first, the children may be clumsy and noisy, but this phase initiates the growth toward more thoughtful creation.

Some child may want to tell the story of Noah and the ark in a few words of his own, as he has heard it. This should be encouraged. Then, all of the children will find the story on pages 12 and 13 an additional listening experience as the teacher reads it or tells it. The story in this book has been purposely written to stimulate more imagery than the biblical story provides. This original story, written in such a way as to suggest the creative dramatics but not to restrict by overinterpretation, will help the children picture the crowding of the animals into the ark, four by four, five by five, six by six, seven by seven, eight by eight, and nine by nine, as the flood waters rise. Suspense is built as the animals climb the mountain to escape the water. One or two pupils could act as the rising water, fluttering behind the group and gently lobbing them ahead.

As the song is acted out, the rush of going into the ark, two by the window and two by the door, and the excitement of Noah's giving directions to his sons about the kinds of food to be put aboard for the different kinds of animals, and finally his "Shut that gate" and "Boys, cut the line," should bring out many original body movements and interpretations.

Now the children begin to see that in a play it is possible to have a great deal of hustle and bustle and seeming confusion without chaos, because of the discussion and planning that went into the production. Each child knows in advance which part he is playing so that he can give his best characterization in controlled interplay with his fellow-actors. Here, a true inner discipline has a chance to develop, based on thinking, and a real exchange of humorous action replaces the undisciplined horseplay so often called "fun."

Use Rimsky-Korsakov's *Flight of the Bumblebee* or Saint-Saëns' *Carnival of the Animals* as additional listening experiences. Again children may have a tendency to use slapstick, if left to interpret these freely. But discussion and guidance by the teacher will cause them to "see" all of the animals in a zoo and "hear" the lions, horses, hens, turtles, elephants, fish, birds, and swans, as the music gives them *word pictures*.

A child may be at the chalkboard sketching one of the animals when the group decides to write a poem. As the teacher draws out the individual "poetic thoughts" of the children, she may find that the composite, based on group choices of the "best" ideas or phrases given verbally by individual children, can often be shaped into a very satisfactory poem. The children will usually give their thoughts in snatches, without concern for rhyme, but they will take great pride in the final poems that they create.

Children should be encouraged to write additional verses for this ballad. Some children will probably discover that certain animals are not mentioned in the song. The teacher might go to the chalkboard and list all of the animals that the children can name. Perhaps the child who names an unfamiliar animal should be asked to explain what the animal looks like. This type of oral expression is an excellent means of forcing children to search for descriptive words.

Children should also be encouraged to draw pictures of animals, as this is another means of creative expression. Since color is important in depicting animals, the children may prefer to do their art work at their desks in order to choose from the wide spectrum of color available in crayons.

While costumes are not absolutely necessary for the dramatization of this ballad, they will add to its ultimate success. An elementary school classroom may have its own costume box. The box will usually contain outgrown or cast-off clothing, which makes excellent costume material. The child playing the part of Noah could wear an old coat and hat. He will certainly want to have a beard, since Noah was a very old man. Because of the many animals involved, *The Story of Noah* provides an opportunity for imaginative costuming. For example, the size of an elephant might suggest the use of pillows stuffed under over-sized clothing. The trunk of the elephant could be made of rolled-up newspaper. Helpful suggestions from the teacher will motivate the children to express their own ideas. Each child can then choose his favorite animal and create his own costume.

Fitting new verses to the music of a song is an excellent means of encouraging young composers and young poets. Rhythm is a basic element of music and poetry. Dividing words into syllables to fit music notation is one of the first steps in composing a song. (This type of syllabification also provides an opportunity for a study of spelling, phonics, and other aspects of the language arts program.)

Related Material

Wild Beasts

I will be a lion
   And you shall be a bear,
And each of us will have a den
   Beneath a nursery chair;
And you must growl and growl and growl,
   And I will roar and roar,
And then — why, then — you'll growl again,
   And I will roar some more!

Evaleen Stein

Jump or Jiggle

Frogs jump
Caterpillars hump

Worms wiggle
Bugs jiggle

Rabbits hop
Horses clop

Snakes slide
Seagulls glide

Mice creep
Deer leap

Puppies bounce
Kittens pounce

Lions stalk
But —
   I walk!

Evelyn Beyer

The Story of Noah

With humor

1. Now did-n't old No-ah build an Ark? Built it out of hick-o-ry bark. Oh, an-i-mals come in one by one, Cow a-chew-in' on a car-a-way bun.

Refrain

Oh, who built the Ark? No-ah built it. Who built the Ark? Old

No-ah built it. Who built the Ark? Old No-ah built it, Cut-tin' his — tim-bers down. —

2. Oh, animals come in two by two,
   Rhinoceros and the kangaroo.
   Oh, animals come in three by three,
   Bear a-huggin' on a bumble-y bee.

   Refrain:

3. Oh, animals come in four by four,
   Two by the window and two by the door.
   Oh, animals come in five by five,
   Thus those animals did arrive.

   Refrain:

4. Oh, animals come in six by six,
   Hyena laughin' at the monkey's tricks.
   Oh, animals come in seven by seven,
   Says the ant to the elephant, "Who is you shovin'?"

   Refrain:

5. Oh, animals come in eight by eight,
   Noah shouted, "Boys, shut that gate!"
   Oh, animals come in nine by nine,
   Noah hollered, "Boys, cut the the line!"

   Refrain:

Who Killed Cock Robin?

One of the first signs of spring is the appearance of a red-breasted bird called a robin. He is such a cocky bird that he is often called by his nickname, Cock Robin. He likes to strut on the lawn, stop, stomp his foot, and cock his head to listen for worms and insects that may be moving in the ground. If he hears anything, he will dip his beak into the ground and often capture a crunchy beetle or a juicy worm.

One winter the weather had been very cold, but Cock Robin started his usual journey to his northern home. As he flew northward, the wind became colder and colder. Finally, when he reached his northern home, he discovered that Jack Frost was still around. Cock Robin felt very cold and looked for a warm place to rest. He knew he could not build a nest in the tree yet, for Jack Frost had touched all the branches with his icy fingers, and the reeds and grasses were caught fast in the hard ground. Jack Frost was his enemy. Cock Robin was afraid.

"I should have waited a few more days to fly north," said Cock Robin to himself as he searched for a place to rest. He flew about until he grew very tired. He fluttered to the ground, hopped into a small clump of dead leaves, and fell asleep.

Early the next morning, the sun came out very bright. It sent Jack Frost fleeing to the North. The weather became warm and pleasant. About the middle of the morning, the sparrow went out hunting for food with his little bow and arrow. He flew in darts and circles near the ground. He thought he saw something red in a clump of leaves. "Now what could that be?" he asked himself. He landed and hopped closer. It was the robin with his head tucked under his wing. "Well, good morning, Cock Robin!" called the sparrow. Cock Robin did not move or make an answer. The sparrow knew that something was wrong, and he stepped closer and closer. Suddenly he realized that Cock Robin was dead! "Who in the world would kill a bird as friendly as Cock Robin?" said the sparrow. "I must go quickly and tell the other birds!" He dropped his bow and arrow and flew away, not even seeing the green-eyed fly who hovered over the grasses nearby.

All of the birds were sorry to hear that Cock Robin was dead. They began asking the same questions the sparrow had asked himself, but they could not find an answer. They decided to bury Cock Robin near the tuft of grass where the sparrow had found him.

The crow came and dug a grave with his grubbing hoe.

The skylark hauled Cock Robin's body to the grave with a horse and cart.

The man-drake smoothed the grave over with his little rake.

The dove preached the sermon. He reminded the birds that Cock Robin had been a friendly bird who was always kind and cheerful. Some of the birds were very sorry that they had been grumpy. The crow and the blue jay resolved that they would stop fussing and fighting with the other birds.

A few days after Cock Robin was buried, the wild flowers began to bloom and the trees put out new buds. It had been such a long winter! The people in the village were really glad to see and feel the warm sun. They missed Cock Robin. Why was he so late in coming this year? They began to ask if anyone had seen him. Finally, they learned that Cock Robin was dead. The sparrow told them how he had found Cock Robin and how the birds had come together to bury him. Nobody seemed to know who killed Cock Robin. Some people thought that the sparrow did it with his bow and arrow. Other people accused the green fly with the sharp eye. Actually, no one ever knew exactly what happened to Cock Robin. His death was such a mystery that it became a legend. Someone even wrote a sad song about it. In fact, if you should go to that village today, you would still hear some of the people singing *Who Killed Cock Robin?*

Teaching Suggestions for "Who Killed Cock Robin?"

Background of the Ballad

This nursery rhyme was probably a political lampoon in England during the eighteenth century; however, the legend itself has roots going as far back as Norse mythology. It may have been connected with renewal-of-the-year ceremonies in which the robin and the wren were sacrificed. Such ceremonies are still performed in some northern European countries.

The first printed version of this rhyme seems to have appeared in 1744. Many variants have been published since that date. Some early illustrations show all the birds weeping and applying handkerchiefs to their eyes. The song is sometimes used as a play-game in which the children hold court. Thus, it becomes a kind of bird detective story.

How to Dramatize

This folk ballad is adaptable to creative dramatics at several different age levels. Since the advent of television, children are well acquainted with court trials and the general meaning of such terms as "circumstantial evidence." Therefore, it might be interesting for the children to reconstruct a trial about this ballad. There would be no limit to the number of birds and crawling or flying things that might make up the audience in the courtroom or serve on the jury. The traits and habits of the different birds "tried" for the murder of Cock Robin might contribute to the evidence. The influence of personal attitudes and prejudices (e.g., "a bird you like" and "a bird you do not like") as expressed by witnesses, jury, and courtroom observers could provide understandings of great significance to children.

From the sound of the music, the children will immediately notice that this is a sad song. Of course, the story itself is sad; therefore, it is fitting for the music to be in a minor key. In the upper grades, children will be able to study and understand the construction of minor scales.

In the lower grades, however, it would be sufficient to explain that a minor key is often used to create a sad feeling in music.

Having heard the recording of the ballad about Cock Robin, the children might be asked to write their own version of this song. Younger children will tell the teacher their versions for her to place on the chalkboard or on experience charts. Since all children derive much pleasure from hearing their own stories and dialogue read aloud, there is reason for allowing written dialogue in some creative dramatics sessions, although the actual replaying of the story and song should not become a "memorized performance." For some groups, such writing leads to more involvement in characterization and helps develop more complex speech habits when the actual "acting out" begins. Awareness of "actable" ideas can be increased through various classroom techniques to remind children of the dramatic possibilities and sources to be found daily in their lives.

Through this activity of writing their own version of the story or song, children will begin to see the inherent dramatic potential in other books and stories and songs. The scarcity of literary plays for elementary school children causes this "making of plays" by children themselves to become a necessity.

At first, it may be difficult for the group to create something different each time the play is acted out; however, they will gradually feel the impulse of creativity. It is the same with pantomime done by little children; at first it is imitative, but after a while the movements and facial expressions come from within, resulting from personalized thoughts and feelings.

The teacher should be sure that the children understand the meaning of all of the new words that are used in the story and song about Cock Robin. Examples of such words and phrases are nickname, grave, resolved, grubbing, mound, sermon, hovered, legend, and tuft of grass. There may be other words throughout this book which will be new to some children. Discussing and understanding the use of these words is an excellent way to build a child's vocabulary.

The habits and characteristics of birds should be discussed thoroughly. The teacher should explain that the man-drake mentioned in the ballad is the male opposite to a duck. Children will think of many ways to breathe and sound and move like the birds and other living creatures that might be included in this ballad. As the child takes on the new identity, he selects appropriate dramatic material out of his experience and knowledge. As members of the group recognize the originality of the characterization, personality interplay begins to occur spontaneously.

The children will enjoy making costumes and props to use in dramatizing this ballad. Many teachers find it helpful to have a costume box which can be added to from time to time if children are encouraged to bring old clothes and costumes from home. A wide variety of colorful clothes can be used if the children decide that they would like to wear costumes in acting out this ballad. A bright orange-red sweater or vest should be worn by the child who plays the role of Cock Robin. All of the birds may be costumed by placing colored paper bags over the children's heads. To facilitate breathing, large holes should be cut for the eyes, nose, and mouth. Colorful top pieces, representing feathers, can be made of paper and attached to the top of the paper bags with staples or glue.

This ballad could be staged outside on the playground or in the classroom with very few stage properties.

Related Material

The following variant of this old nursery rhyme might provide additional ideas for acting it out.

The Death and Burial of Cock Robin

Who killed Cock Robin?
"I," said the Sparrow,
"With my bow and arrow,
I killed Cock Robin."

Who saw him die?
"I," said the Fly,
"With my little eye,
I saw him die."

Who caught his blood?
"I," said the Fish,
"With my little dish,
I caught his blood."

Who'll make his shroud?
"I," said the Beetle,
"With my thread and needle,
I'll make his shroud."

Who'll dig his grave?
"I," said the Owl,
"With my spade and trowel,
I'll dig his grave."

Who'll be the parson?
"I," said the Rook,
"With my little book,
I'll be the parson."

Who'll be the clerk?
"I," said the Lark,
"If it's not in the dark;
I'll be the clerk."

Who'll be chief mourner?
"I," said the Dove,
"I mourn for my love;
I'll be chief mourner."

Who'll bear the torch?
"I," said the Linnet,
"I'll come in a minute;
I'll bear the torch."

Who'll sing his dirge?
"I," said the Thrush,
As she sat in a bush,
"I'll sing his dirge."

Who'll bear the pall?
"We," said the Wren,
Both the Cock and the Hen;
"We'll bear the pall."

Who'll carry his coffin?
"I," said the Kite,
"If it's not in the night,
I'll carry his coffin."

Who'll toll the bell?
"I," said the Bull,
"Because I can pull,
I'll toll the bell."

All the birds of the air
Fell to singing and sobbing
When they heard the bell toll
For poor Cock Robin.
Anonymous

Who Killed Cock Robin?

2. Who dug his grave?
   It must have been a black crow.
   Who dug his grave?
   It must have been a black crow.
   Who dug his grave?
   It must have been a black crow
   With his little grubbing hoe.
   Who hauled him to it?
   It must have been a skylark.
   Who hauled him to it?
   It must have been a skylark.
   Who hauled him to it?
   It must have been a skylark
   With his little horse and cart.

3. Who smoothed his mound o'er?
   It must have been a man-drake.
   Who smoothed his mound o'er?
   It must have been a man-drake.
   Who smoothed his mound o'er?
   It must have been a man-drake
   'Cause he's got a little rake.
   Who preached the sermon?
   It must have been a mourning dove.
   Who preached the sermon?
   It must have been a mourning dove.
   Who preached the sermon?
   It must have been a mourning dove,
   And he said it out of love.

Posheen, Posheen, Posho

Once there was a little mouse town called Posheen. The town was located between the rows in a big cornfield. The homes were up on the hills on both sides of the dirt road that ran between the rows of corn. It was a pleasant little town, full of nice friendly mice. They were proud of their community, but some of the leading citizens thought the roads were getting in bad shape. They decided to take their complaints to the mayor, Mr. Joe Mouse. Many mice thought that Mr. Joe was getting too old to look after the roads. It was almost time for another election, so Mr. Joe promised to make an immediate inspection of all roads and tunnels.

As Mr. Joe walked through the village roads, he overheard some of the younger mice say how old and feeble he looked. He did not like this a bit. He knew that he would have to be spry to hold on to his job. He stopped, slicked up his shiny gray coat, combed his moustache, and began to scamper down the road.

Mr. Joe looked up and down each row of streets. "These streets look pretty good to me," he mumbled to himself.

As he drew near the cheese factory, he stood up straight to sniff the air. He felt so good that he tried to hop along, but standing up straight, he could not see where he was going. Suddenly —— oof! —— he stubbed his toe on a big clod of dirt. "My, these roads do need some work," he moaned.

As he hobbled on down the road, his toe began to swell and ache. How he wished for a bandage! Suddenly, he spied a blue silk ribbon. "This will have to do in place of a bandage," he said. He stopped and wrapped up his toe in the blue silk ribbon.

Then he started down the road again, with every step causing great pain. About this time, little Susie Mouse came walking by with her grandmother. Susie was from Posho, a mouse town about twenty rows from Posheen. She was visiting her grandmother and had come out to help her pick up grains of corn. But she was also looking for a blue hair ribbon she had lost the day before.

Since little Susie was only visiting in Posheen, she had never seen Mr. Joe Mouse. She did not know he was a very old and respected citizen of Posheen, much less the *mayor*. When she looked down and saw his toe all bandaged up with her blue silk ribbon, she began to shake with laughter. She laughed so much that she could not hear Mr. Joe groaning with pain. Her grandmother grew very angry and told Susie she should be ashamed to laugh at Mr. Joe. But Susie was laughing so hard that she could not stop. Her granny reached up and plucked a stem of yellow broom corn and gave little Susie a good spanking. Of course, this made Susie stop laughing!

Mr. Joe was still in awful pain, but now his pride was hurt even more than his toe. When little Susie saw how sad he was, she went over and said, "Mr. Joe, I want to apologize for laughing when you are in such pain. I was not really laughing at you, but at that bandage on your toe. That is the blue silk ribbon I wear in my hair. I lost it yesterday when I was helping grandmother pick up corn."

"Well," said Mr. Joe, "I guess I do look silly with this big blue ribbon on my toe." Mr. Joe began to laugh at himself. In fact, he laughed so hard that he forgot the pain. He took the ribbon from his toe and gave it back to Susie. "Thanks for the use of the ribbon," Mr. Joe said to Susie. "This is election year, so I'd better be about my business of inspecting the streets. I'll see that the road from Posheen to Posho is kept in good shape so that you can visit with your grandmother as often as you wish."

Teaching Suggestions for "Posheen, Posheen, Posho"

Mr. Niles discovered this song from an old woman in North Carolina. She used the word "gammer" for grandmother, which gives the ballad an air of antiquity. It should be remembered that *Gammer Gurton's Needle* was one of the first plays printed in English, predating Shakespeare by many years.

The word "posheen" is probably Gaelic in origin. Here it is used as a nonsense word.

How to Dramatize

Teachers will probably be surprised at the popularity of this folk ballad. The authors discovered that the bandaged foot and other actions of the characters are uproariously funny to children. The very words "posheen" and "posho" are humorous, and the contrast of the minor key in the tune seems to heighten the mood. Children have been observed using this song as a playground folk game.

The more imaginative and nonsensical the rhyme, the freer the young child will be to project his emotions into the body or shape or environment of something or someone other than himself. The children may want to add extra scenes to this play, so the teacher will say, "Posheen, Posheen, Posho, did you stub your toe?" which will mean it is the child's turn to think of another funny story to act out.

After the children have heard the story, the teacher may think of other ways to build interest. She may want the children to draw their own pictures of the man-mouse with the bandaged toe, or of the mice scurrying along between the corn rows. (If the story told on pages 24 and 25 is used, the teacher may wish the children to draw pictures of each character, and of the houses in the town of Posheen.) Having heard the record, the children will be repeating the words of the poem. Allow

them to speak the words of the song many times before they sing it, exaggerating the p's, m's, and b's. Some will have become very good at the laughing, "Ho ho ho ho ho ho ho ho," way down deep in their stomachs, or way up high in their heads like a very squeaky mouse. Some will have tried the range of high to low, low to high.

Costumes and properties are not essential to the success of creative dramatics. Usually the children can pantomime even the props, and they can "feel" that they are in the garb of someone else. However, sometimes a simple prop will add much to the fun. In this case, materials for tying up the toe, and a piece of rolled-up newspaper or oak-tag paper for the spanking, are almost a must.

Some questions and suggestions from the teacher will guide the children quickly into the action. First comes the selection of the characters. The part of the grandmother will be much sought after by both boys and girls. Since there are only three main characters in this song, the children may want to act it out several times. If the story on pages 24 and 25 excites interest, perhaps the children will want to bring in additional characters, such as the mice who complained about the bad roads, and the young mice who said Mr. Joe was getting old.

Whenever evaluation takes place, it would be better to discuss the character, not the child playing the character. For example, "Was the girl-mouse just acting silly that time?" rather than "Was Jane acting silly that time?" Even in simple creations like this, children can learn that it is more fun to control the character, to be a funny *actor*, not a funny Jane! Later on, as they attempt more difficult characterizations, some discipline will have been achieved from within.

The timid child is often a problem. Even in simple dramatics, he must be encouraged to try a part. The aggressive children may further inhibit the shy ones. Even with excellent questioning on the part of the teacher, some children cannot change the image they have of themselves. Through just one simple group activity, such children will be helped toward self-expression in other areas. One first-grader had been completely nonsocial and uncommunicative until the day the music teacher placed a pair of maracas in his hands while the class was singing a rhythmic song. He simply followed the rhythm. From that moment, he was cooperative with the teacher and more sociable with the other children.

The objective for this and other creative dramatics experiences is the individual and social development of every child who participates.

Related Material

The teacher may draw on the knowledge of children for songs and poems that can be related to this unit. For example, some children will likely suggest singing the nursery rhyme *Hickory Dickory Dock*. Or, the children may want to make up their own music to go with the following rhyme:

A Chinese Nursery Rhyme

He ran up the candlestick
The little mousey brown,
To steal and eat tallow,
And he couldn't get down.

He called for his grandma,
But his grandma was in town;
So he doubled up into a wheel
And rolled himself down.

Translated by I. T. Headland

Another related poem may lead to more study of animal habits, especially of the mouse.

The City Mouse and the Garden Mouse

The city mouse lives in a house;
The garden mouse lives in a bower,
He's friendly with the frogs and toads,
And sees the pretty plants in flower.

The city mouse eats bread and cheese;
The garden mouse eats what he can;
We will not grudge him seeds and stocks,
Poor little timid furry man.

Christina Georgina Rossetti

Guitar accompaniments would be very appropriate for all of the folk ballads in this book. Guitar fingering for all the chords in the ballads are given below:

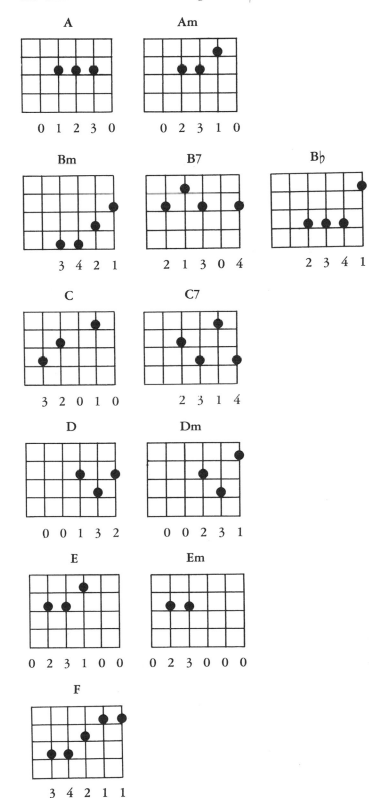

Posheen, Posheen, Posho

Sadly, with humor

1. Po - sheen, po - sheen, po - sho._____ A man-mouse stubbed__ his toe._____ He wrapped it up with a cot - ton band And made it fast with a blue silk strand, Po - sheen, po-sheen, po - sho._____ sho._____

2. Posheen, posheen, posho,
   A girl-mouse laughèd so
   To see a man-mouse with a wrappèd up toe.
   She laughed ho, ho, ho, ho, ho, ho, ho,
   Posheen, posheen, posho.

3. Posheen posheen, posho.
   Her granny was angered so.
   She plucked a stem of yellow broom corn
   And with a will she laid it on,
   Posheen, posheen, posho.

History of the Folk Ballad

"A ballad is a song that tells a story, or to take it from the other point of view, a story told in song." This is one of the best-known and most widely accepted definitions in all of ballad study. It is the opening statement of the Preface to the *English and Scottish Popular Ballads,* collected and edited by Francis James Child. (The Preface, however, was written by his associate, G. L. Kittredge.)

The plot of the story told in a ballad is usually very simple, and the material developed around it becomes a narrative poem. In present-day times, the poem of the ballad is thought to represent one-half of the unit, the music and the singing thereof representing the other half. Unfortunately, this was not always so, for as ballad singing in England declined, either the ballad poem was read (rather than sung) or the entire ballad was forgotten. About fifty years ago, the great English ballad authority, Cecil Sharp, was convinced that the ballad was dead. According to him, "Nobody sings the old songs any more." A few years later this same Cecil Sharp had to admit his error, because he discovered that in the Southern Appalachian region here in America, the ballad was being sung by native singers. If Cecil Sharp were living today, he would discover — to his pleasure, we hope — that our country is in the midst of a widespread ballad and folk song revival. This renewed interest in folk singing is spreading to many areas — school, home, and concert hall. The ballad, to which authorship is not usually claimed, has once more taken its rightful place in the area of poetry and music.

Any song which tells a story can be called a ballad; yet, a "classic" ballad is one which goes back to authenticated English and Scottish sources. Generally speaking, a classic ballad in American oral tradition has its counterpart in Francis J. Child's monumental collection, compiled from written sources in the British Isles. Thus, the ballad of *John Henry* is not a classic, but *Barbara Allen* is. A classic ballad has no known author, and the person singing the ballad might be classed as the author quite as well as the unknown bard who first made the idea rhyme. Many folk singers believe that the only sure way to present the ballad convincingly is to sing the story as if it were being made up on the spot. Then it has vigor and freshness. It is this self-renewing vitality which is at the base of the folk song revival of our times.

This, too, is the reason why folk music is so effective as creative dramatics material for young children. The freshness and vitality of this music is preserved because children believe that what they are singing or saying is a story being created for the first time. As they sing and act out their own folk music, these children become a part of a native culture arising from the language they speak and the country to which they belong.

It should be pointed out that the ballads in this book are not among the classics, although two of them, *Cock Robin* and *The Frog in the Spring*, go back into early times. They have no counterparts in Francis J. Child's collection. *The Story of Noah*, based on the biblical story, is obviously an American product. The origin of *Posheen, Posheen, Posho* is unknown. All four of these songs are properly classified as ballads because each of them tells a story. Storytelling was a vastly important enterprise before radio, television, and mass-produced books made it possible to delegate storytelling to experts.

Ballad poetry and music flourished side by side in long-ago times, but with the advent of Oliver Cromwell the ballad was banned because of political connotations. In cities, ballads were sung in secret, if at all; however, the country people kept the ballad alive. Of course soldiers, sailors, and a few great scholars continued their constant interest in the ballad.

It was many years before ballad singing returned to the English scene, and then the return was a timid one. In America, however, timidity was not the order of the day. Ballad singing became vitally interwoven into the lives of our pioneer ancestors. They promptly forgot ballads concerning historical events which did not concern them in the New World. Those ballads which remained in their memories of Old England were concerned with love, family tragedy, adventure, and death. Some of the ballads were adapted or completely changed to fit the emerging American culture.

Education was not easily acquired in our pioneer days, and many of the early settlers in the southern mountains were unable to read. What culture they had was a remembered thing. Cecil Sharp once said, "That the illiterate may nevertheless reach a high level of culture will surprise those only who imagine that education and civilization are convertible terms." The uneducated rural man, depending on some inner source of power to sustain him in his difficult moments, will develop his memory of things long past. He will recall diversions or events of one kind or another and color them with philosophy, humor, and provincial expressions.

This is exactly what happened to the fine old English ballads in the hands of our pioneer ancestors, and our children today seem to sense the genuine poetry of the ballads they have inherited. At the same time, these children will react with less enthusiasm to the more obviously contrived and manufactured ballads.

A ballad is a song that tells a story, and the retelling of stories by way of singing is so deeply ingrained in the American scene that new ballads are being created. Whether these new ballads will stand the test of time remains to be seen. Their fate will depend on whether they are sufficiently direct, simple, and powerful, and whether their themes have universal appeal. The old ballads have passed their test. Their very existence is the proof of their validity.

Bibliography for Creative Dramatics

Allstrom, Elizabeth. *Let's Play a Story*. New York: Friendship Press, 1957.

Andrews, Gladys. *Creative Rhythmic Movement for Children*. Englewood Cliffs, N.J.: Prentice-Hall, Inc., 1954.

Burger, Isabel. *Creative Play Acting*. New York: A. S. Barnes and Co., 1950.

Durland, Frances Caldwell. *Creative Dramatics for Children*. Yellow Springs, Ohio: The Antioch Press, 1952.

Hartley, Eugene E. *Understanding Children's Play*. New York: The Columbia University Press, 1952.

Landeck, Beatrice. *Songs to Grow On*. New York: Edward B. Marks Music Corporation, 1950.

Lease, Ruth C., and Siks, Geraldine Brain. *Creative Dramatics for Home, School, and Community*. New York: Harper and Brothers, 1952.

National Education Association, Elementary Instructional Service. *Creative Dramatics* (pamphlet). Washington, D.C.: March, 1959.

———. *Storytelling and the Teacher* (pamphlet). Washington, D.C.: March, 1960.

National Education Association, Music Educators National Conference. *Music in Everyday Living and Learning*. Washington, D.C.: 1960.

Ritchie, Jean. *The Swapping Song Book*. New York: Oxford University Press, Inc., 1952.

Sheehy, Emma D. *Children Discover Music and Dance*. New York: Holt, Rinehart and Winston, Inc., 1959.

Siks, Geraldine Brain, and Dunnington, Hazel Brain. *Children's Theatre and Creative Dramatics*. Seattle: University of Washington Press, 1961.

Siks, Geraldine Brain. *Creative Dramatics: An Art for Children*. New York: Harper and Brothers, 1958.

Ward, Winifred. *Playmaking with Children*, rev. ed. New York: Appleton-Century-Crofts, Inc., 1957.